i live in music

poem by ntozake shange
paintings by romare bearden

edited by linda sunshine
designed by eric baker

a welcome book

distributed by

stewart, tabori & chang, inc.

i live in music

is this where you live

i live here in music

i live on c♯ street

my friend lives on b♭ avenue

do you live here in music

sound

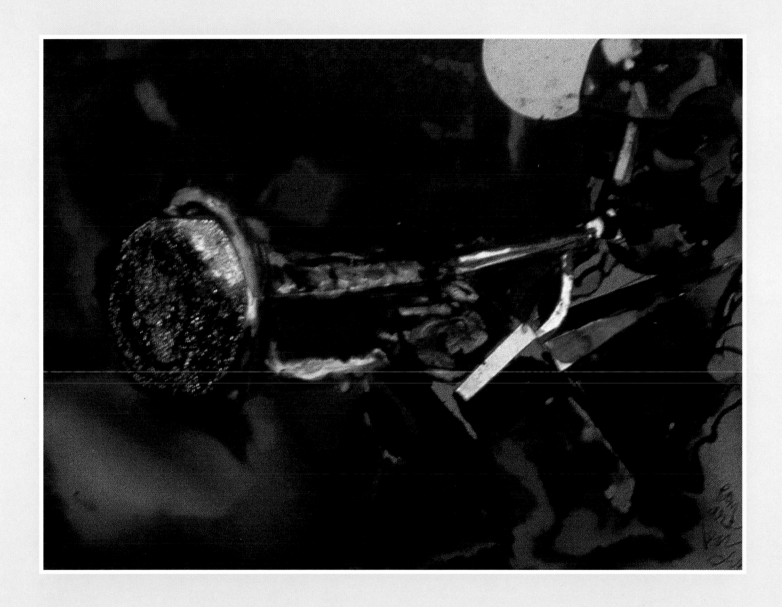

falls round me like rain on other folks

saxophones wet my face

hot like peppers i rub on my lips
thinkin they waz lilies

i got 15 trumpets where other women got hips

& a upright bass for both sides of my heart

i walk round in a piano like somebody else/ be walkin on the earth

i live in music
live in it
wash in it

i cd even smell it
wear sound on my fingers

sound falls

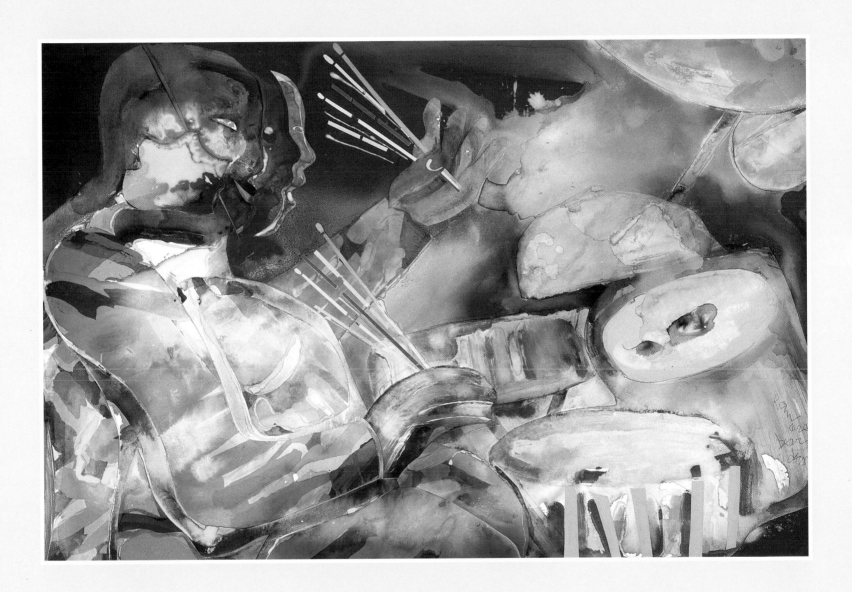

so fulla music

ya cd make a river where yr arm is &
hold yrself

hold yrself in a music

i live in music

i live in music
is this where you live
i live here in music
i live on c♯ street
my friend lives on b♭ avenue
do you live here in music
sound
falls round me like rain on other folks
saxophones wet my face
cold as winter in st. louis
hot like peppers i rub on my lips
thinkin they waz lilies
i got 15 trumpets where other women got hips
& a upright bass for both sides of my heart
i walk round in a piano like somebody
else/ be walkin on the earth
i live in music

    live in it

        wash in it

i cd even smell it
wear sound on my fingers
sound falls   so fulla music
ya cd make a river where yr arm is &
hold yrself

        hold yrself in a music

Ntozake Shange

An accomplished musician and a professional actress and dancer, as well as a writer, Ntozake Shange was born Paulette Williams in Trenton, New Jersey in 1948 and grew up in St. Louis, the setting for her second novel, *Betsey Brown*. She now lives in Philadelphia. Her father is a physician and her mother is a social worker and teacher.

Ms. Shange graduated in 1970 from Barnard College and took a Masters Degree in English Literature from UCLA. She was thrown into the national limelight during the 1970s when her choreo-poem, *for colored girls—who have considered suicide/when the rainbow is enuf*, was produced in New York both off and on Broadway with spectacular success. Since that time she's written and had produced four more plays including "*I heard eric dolphy in his eyes*," "*The Love Space Demands: A Continuing Saga*" and an adaptation of *Mother Courage*. Ms. Shange also adapted *Betsey Brown* to *Betsey Brown: A Rhythm & Blues Musical* which opened in the spring of 1991. Her other published works include *Sassafras, Cypress & Indigo, Spell #7*, "*A Photograph: Lovers in Motion*" and the poetry volumes, *nappy edges, A Daughter's Geography, Ridin' the Moon in Texas* and *From Okra to Greens*.

Of her ongoing work Shange says that while many, maybe most, writers think of literature as a written art object, she herself came to language, poetry and music both in an oral and aural tradition in English, Spanish and French, and it never occurred to her to try to separate or disengage one from the other. Thus, among many other poems and prose pieces, she has performed and recorded *i live in music* with her band, Syllable.

Ms. Shange has also worked and performed with innumerable artists including Dianne McIntyre's Sounds-in-Motion, Raymond Sawyer's Afro-Asian Dance Company, Ed Mock's West Coast Dance Works and The Stanze Peterson Dance Company, as well as many individual musicians. Tapes of her recordings are available through The San Francisco State University Poetry Center and Audio Prose Library Inc. in Columbia, Missouri.

Ms. Shange's column appears regularly in Philadelphia's *Real News* and her articles and poetry may be found in *Uncut Funk, Callaloo, Muleteeth* and *Essence*. Her most recent novel is *Liliane: Resurrection of the Daughter*.

Romare Bearden

"I think the artist has to be something like a whale," Romare Bearden once said, "swimming with his mouth wide open, absorbing everything until he has what he really needs. When he finds that, he can start to make limitations. And then he really begins to grow."

One of America's pre-eminent artists, Romare Bearden (1912-1988) was born in North Carolina, raised in Harlem and Pittsburgh, studied in Paris and lived in New York and St. Martin. He made his name in the art world, showing with Robert Motherwell, William Baziotes and Carl Holty in the 1940s; had a career in songwriting in the 1950s (Billy Eckstein and Dizzy Gillespie recorded *Seabreeze*, Bearden's one big hit) and turned almost exclusively to collage, a medium he re-invented with singular success, by the early 1960s. "I paint out of the tradition of the blues, of call and recall. You start a theme and you call and recall," Romare Bearden said. "You must become a blues singer—only you sing on the canvas. You improvise—you find the rhythm and catch it good and structure it as you go along—then the song is you."

Today, Bearden's works are in the collections of every major museum in New York City as well as more than a dozen across the country. President Carter honored Mr. Bearden and nine other visual artists in 1980. Bearden was awarded a National Medal of Arts from President Reagan in 1987. A former member of the American Institute of Arts and Letters, Romare Bearden was a member of the board of the New York State Council of the Arts when he died in 1988.

When asked to describe the main themes of his work, Bearden told an interviewer, "the land, the beauty of the black woman, the protective presence of the dead and the acceptance of intuition." But others have expanded on his range. Ralph Ellison wrote that Bearden's "combination of techniques is in itself eloquent of the sharp breaks, leaps of consciousness, distortions, paradoxes, reversals, telescoping of time and surreal blending of styles, values, hopes and dreams which characterize much of Negro American history."

Published books of his art include: *Romare Bearden: His Life and Art* by Myron Schwartzman (Abrams, 1990); *Romare Bearden* by Lowery Stokes Sims (Rizzoli, 1993) and *Romare Bearden: A Memorial Exhibition* (ACA Galleries, 1989). Along with Harry Henderson, he is the co-author of *A History of African-American Artists* (Pantheon, 1994), an extensive study which took twenty years to compile and was published posthumously in February of 1994.

The editor would like to thank Gregory Perrin, Mrs. Nanette Rohan Bearden, Michael Denneny, and Alison Hagge for their help with this book.

Published by Welcome Enterprises, Inc., 575 Broadway, New York, NY 10012

Distributed by Stewart, Tabori & Chang, 575 Broadway, New York, NY 10012

Distributed in Canada by General Publishing Co. Ltd., 20 Lesmill Road, Don Mills, Ontario, Canada M3B2T6

Library of Congress
Cataloging-in-Publication Data
Shange, Ntozake.
    I live in music / poem by Ntozake Shange ; paintings by Romare Bearden ; edited by Linda Sunshine.
        p. cm.
    ISBN 1-55670-372-4 : $15.95
    1. Music--Poetry.   I. Bearden, Romare, 1911–1988.   II. Sunshine, Linda.   III. Title.
    PS3569.H3324I2   1994
    811' .54--dc20   94-18565
                                              CIP